The Fairy Gala

Community Includes Everyone.

Martha Begley Schade

Martha Begley Schade, Galway, Ireland

Illustrated edition published in Ireland in 2022

Title: The Fairy Gala. Community Includes Everyone.

This book is a work of fiction and tells the story of a Fairy Gala that takes place in Merlin Woods. It shows how the fairies work together to achieve great things.

Registered with Nielsen Pubeasy where you can order this book or, alternatively, you can contact the author herself at marthabegleybooks@gmail.com. Or via www.galwayfairytales.com

Medical Disclaimer: This publication is meant as a source of valuable information for the reader, however it is not meant as a substitute for direct expert assistance. If such level of assistance is required, the services of a competent professional should be sought.

Illustrations created by Ishara Kavinda Thilakarathna

First Edition.

ISBN 978-1-83801485-8

Table of Contents

Introduction

et me tell you a story about one of the most special events ever witnessed in Merlin Woods. It was late afternoon on a lovely spring day and a warm and gentle breeze was blowing. Just as well too, as Síofra was very hot about the collar trying to get everything ready. She had the fairies all doing little jobs.

Siofra looked down at the checklist she was holding. Colourful bunting hung gaily from the trees.

Vibrantly colourful flags waved magically in the breeze.

The hearty aroma of delicious dishes prepared with love wafted through the air. The lush smell of fresh berries and fruit was mouth-watering.

The canopy of the trees was silhouetted on the ground, with shadows cast by floating lanterns.

The paths were marked by invisible signs that only the fairies could see, pointing in the direction of where the gala events were to be held. A polished trophy reflected the oncoming dusk, brighter than a mirror.

She frowned as she checked the long list one last time and then looked up with a smile on her face.

"Yes, I think we are ready at last", she said, beaming at her young fairies. "Now, you all need to hurry up and get ready. The others will be arriving soon".

Who did she mean you may ask? You see, scores of fairies from other places were due to arrive to celebrate the great Fairy Gala. As this only took place once in a hundred years, it was a celebration not to be missed. As this year it was going to be hosted in Merlin Woods, Síofra naturally wanted everything to look spectacular, to set the scene for a bright and memorable experience. With that, they all flew to their homes, happy and excited about this marvellous event which would take place the very next day.

The Day Arrives

Naoise was helping Willow to do her hair. "Oh Willow, this is just so exciting. I hope it will all work out just as we've planned".

"Hurry up, Naoise. They should be arriving very soon and I want to be there to see them", Willow said, keen for her to finish quickly.

"There now! You look beautiful." Naoise said as she gave her a final pat on the head. "Let's go down to the stream. I think that's where it will all be happening. Come on, I don't want to be the last or miss anything. I wonder what the other fairies look like".

With that, they both whizzed off, flying as fast as they could to join the others. Just in time too, because they could hear the loud flapping of an incoming swan with its passengers.

The excitement was great as they all watched a large and seriously graceful white swan circle above them until it finally came into land, spreading its powerful wings and lowering its legs. On its back it carried the fairies hailing from Coole Park.

The swan nestled into the ground to allow the fairies to

disembark by sliding along her wings. Six fairies now stood in a row with their fairy teacher in a fine display.

The Merlin Woods fairies couldn't believe their eyes. Even though it was frightfully bad manners, they couldn't help gawping.

These fairies were all men! Dressed in quaint outfits, they carried stylish handbags and sported dandy hairstyles.

Síofra gave her folks one of those looks, the kind of frown that frazzles, makes you want to run away and hide. "Come on, girls!" she said. "Give your guests a proper welcome to Merlin Woods".

Naoise and Willow stepped forward with the others. This was just too strange for words. How were they supposed to act?

"Welcome to Merlin Woods", gulped Trish, one of the Merlin Woods fairies. "I hope you enjoy your time with us", and, with that, she reached out a welcoming hand.

Having broken the ice, the others soon followed suit.

It was when the Coole Park team started to empty their handbags onto the grass that all the Merlin team regained their composure, along with their sense of fun and excitement. Out of the handbags came the most awesome crew of ladybirds and spiders you have ever seen. They had brought their pets with them for luck!

Soon the Merlin Team and the Coole Park team were chuckling and laughing together as they fed the weird assortment of pets and played with them.

The Other Teams Arrive

Not long afterwards they heard a loud whirring noise. Coming in to land was a gigantic grasshopper which also flew wide of the mark and then finally settled on the grass. Crouching down low, it deposited the strangest set of fairies on the ground.

Once again, the Merlin Fairies stood rooted in utter astonishment. But this time, they weren't alone. The fairies from Coole Park joined them.

Descending from the back of the grasshopper were six fairies, six fairies in all and they were green all over, skin, hair, nails and so on! Zero other colours, just green! And their clothes? Ragged, in tatters! What a strange way to come to such an event.

Once again Síofra had to break the stunned silence. She glided forward, beckoning to the others to do the same. Together they welcomed the strange green creatures from Barna Woods. Indeed, a sight to behold!

Naoise turned to Willow: "Gosh", she said, "this is all a lot weirder than I expected. I thought the Barna crowd would have at least made the effort to put on some decent clothes".

The group stood looking at each other, with one or other of them attempting to strike up a conversation.

Suddenly the drumbeat of loud wings flapping broke the rather awkward silence.

Looking up, they saw the beautiful wingspan of an owl as he soared in to land. A cheer went up. It was Tristan, Merlin Wood's very own owl, and they were so proud of him.

He had offered to fly down to Limerick and transport the fairies from Croom who wanted to take part in the gala.

Tristan had soon deposited his passengers, and six new fairies stood ready to join the others standing in the grass on the fringe of Merlin Woods.

Once again, Síofra reached out to greet the newcomers which was what she had to do. All the others were looking on in stunned amazement as the six little fairies bounced their way over to her.

These fairies had really short bandy legs and instead of walking they seemed to bounce along. Not only that, their wings were unique, unlike any the other fairies had ever seen before.

But what made these Croom fairies really special were their engaging smiles. You couldn't help but like them.

When they smiled, it was catching. You couldn't help but smile back at them.

"Welcome to Merlin Woods!" said Síofra, greeting them warmly. "We are just waiting for one last team to arrive and then we can all go into the woods for refreshments".

Hardly had she finished her sentence when the air around them started to swirl. A look to the skies revealed a spectacular sight.

Seven multi-coloured jewelled butterflies were winging their way towards the grassy area by Merlin Woods where they deposited six fairies from Aranislia and their teacher on the ground.

The others, getting used to all the strange goings-on and feeling better able to handle the situation and more at ease, stepped forward to welcome them. These fairies were odd to say the least.

They waved their hands around a lot, gesturing to each other and communicating more with their eyes. When the fairies listened to them talk, no one could understand a word they were saying!

"Well, after everything we have seen so far, we could hardly have expected them to be normal now could we?" said Willow.

"Hold on a second", said Naoise. "What's normal? Are we normal? Maybe they are they the normal ones and we're not!"

Together, they followed a secret path leading deep into the woods where refreshments were laid out on a banqueting table. Their passage was a sight to behold! Some flew, some walked, and some just bounced along. All a little nervous at having to deal with such differences. This was going to be a gala to be remembered!

The Games Commence

That night, the very second the clock struck midnight, when the full moon emerged from behind the clouds to shed its bright light, the fairies all gathered in a large clearing in the woods to begin the games. The woods were bathed in a soft warm glow.

Síofra stood up and began to speak to the crowd. She explained how the gala was made up of several challenges for the teams to overcome.

This gala was aimed at identifying the team of fairies who had learnt the most about being good fairies during their apprenticeships.

The first challenge, she explained, consisted of surmounting several obstacles she and the elves from Merlin woods had built. Each obstacle would require excellent flying skills and was designed to test them to the utmost – their accuracy and manoeuvrability.

They duly fell into line, ready to take their turn. The Merlin Woods fairies went first. Of course, they did very well. Unknown to Síofra and everyone else, they had sneaked in and practised. They knew where to go fast and where to slow down and take extra care. They had the home advantage.

Next came the Coole Park fairies. They excelled – adept and skillful, they mastered the course in a very short time.

They swooped and swerved their way gracefully past all the obstacles, with their teacher watching them with immense pride.

Next up were the Barna fairies. In their ungainly fashion, they bumped their way around the course. One crashed into a tree, the next missed one of the obstacles completely and had to be disqualified. But it was when the plump fairy got stuck in a hoop that all hell broke loose. So firmly was she wedged all her attempts to wiggle out were in vain.

While some of the fairies watched on in horror, two of the Limerick fairies bounded over to her. One went behind her and shoved hard, the other went to grasp both her hands and then pulled mightily. Several heaves and pushes later she was finally freed.

Tears of shame began to roll down her face and she faltered, unwilling to continue. But all the other fairies started to clap and cheer her on.

Taking heart at their enthusiasm and support, she mustered up enough courage to finish the course.

Síofra and the other teachers looked on, their hearts swelling with pride at their young fairies' performance.

The Limerick team was up next. While three of their fairies got through the course without a hitch, the other three didn't. They experienced quite a few setbacks and lost time by not navigating the curves quickly enough.

The Aranislia team was the last to compete. They did not fare much better but still made sufficiently good time. As each of their team finished their round, loud cries of "Heidizza, hoopla" were to be heard.

Naoise and Willow and a few others as well wondered what this could mean.

"Funny words! What do you think they mean?"

"Gosh" said Naoise, I have no idea. Mumbo jumbo if you ask me."

The Next Challenge

With challenge number one completed, they moved over to the Listening Tree. What a sad sight! There stood a tree that had been split in two by lightning, cleft cleanly right down the middle.

Síofra explained that the next task was to test their powers of healing. She instructed the groups to come up with a way to help the tree which had been struck so hard by lightning.

They had thirty minutes to come up with a solution and then tell everyone their plan.

The teams huddled together in their groups, deliberating on how to fix the tree. They talked animatedly, trying to come up with a solution.

Once the half an hour was up, Síofra invited each of the team leaders to present their ideas.

21

First came the Coole Park team who had decided that special plants around the tree would help.

They would find special herbs, arnica and rosemary, and chamomile, along with wildflowers, daisies, bee orchids and suchlike.

Next came the Aranislian team who felt that seaweed with all its minerals and vitamins packed into the tree's roots would help it flourish and regain its strength, enabling it to recover.

The Merlin Woods team wanted to strip out all the dead wood and unnecessary branches so that the healthy parts could focus on growing again.

The Limerick team who were great musicians thought that playing soft, sweet melodies for the tree would make it happier and give it new life.

It was the Barna team who suggested that wrapping the tree in fine silk thread to hold it together and prevent it from falling apart completely would be the best idea.

Síofra and the teachers listened in amazement to these creative ideas.

Suddenly one of the Limerick team jumped up with delight on her face. "Hey, why don't we try out all of these ideas? Surely, if we all work together we will manage to help the tree?" She grinned from ear to ear, looking eagerly at all the other fairies.

A chorus of "Yes! Of course! Let's do it!" followed and without waiting for their teachers' approval, the fairies sprang into action in unison, keen to fulfil their different tasks.

In no time at all, the tree was no longer split.

It was surrounded by vigorous new plants and seaweed was mixed with the earth and filled out the roots of the tree. The tree had a clean shape to it, like a new haircut – it was as if it could breathe more freely again.

All the while the Limerick musicians played the most exquisite, enchanting music.

But equally magical were the fine silk fibres, in a myriad of colours, which had been spun around the tree by the Barna team. Being so strong a fabric, the silk skeins were holding the tree, forging it back together again.

It was a sight to behold! The fairies stood back to admire their work.

Doubtless a fleeting impression and a flight of fancy, but they thought that they could see the tree gently shake its branches in gratitude and appreciation.

"I'm curious now", said Naoise. "If you can make such wonderful colourful silk in your team, why haven't you designed such exquisite silk clothes for yourselves?" she asked the leader of the Barna team.

"Well, it is like this", the leader said. "We simply don't believe that you need fine silk to be a good fairy! What you wear isn't important for being a good person so we don't bother… but as you can see, we could if we wanted to". She gave Naoise a big wink and sauntered off full of confidence.

Next Challenge

Síofra called to the fairies to gather around while she explained the next challenge. They were to go Merlin Woods Castle where each team would be given an item. Their challenge was to transport the item to the top of the castle without touching it or without entering the castle. The teams went into their various huddles again to discuss how they could best approach this challenge.

"If we only had a picture in our minds of what the top of the castle looks like we could teleport the items", said the leader of the Barna team.

"We could stand on each other's shoulders, form a fairy ladder and ask our ladybirds to climb up with the item", said the Coole Park team.

"Tristan the owl was so kind and accommodating. He could carry it up there for us, couldn't he?" asked the Limerick team.

"There's only one thing for it", said one of the Coole Park team "We will have to use our powers of levitation".

With that, the team from Aranislia stepped forward, murmuring amongst themselves. They started to hum: "Ah-ohm, ah-ohm, ah-kee, ah-lee". Arms stretched out and fingers pointing at the items and with a flutter of their wings, they slowly took to the air.

With that, all the teams' items began to rise too. The hum continued: "Ah-ohm, Ah-ohm, ah-key, ah-key".

The flight of the Aranislians was closely tracked by the items which rose with them. In less than a minute, all items were safely levitated and placed on the roof of the castle.

The Aranislian team returned to the ground, landing daintily to the sound of loud cheering from the other fairies.

"We do not speak as you do – but we are very good at levitating. Na-munbee!"

"Phew! That was great", said one of the Coole Park team. "We don't use levitating where we are so we didn't have a clue how it works. I'm so glad you were here to do it for us!"

And with that, another cheer went up in the crowd and they smiled at each other in delight.

The teachers looked on with bemused. While the outcome of the challenge was not quite what they had planned, there was something so right about what had happened. The teams all pulling together was a fine thing to see.

Then came the Treasure hunt when the fairies had to follow one clue to find the next and so on until the treasure was finally found. The Aranislian team naturally had some difficulties as they didn't understand the clues well enough. But you know what? The other teams jumped in to help them along.

And guess what:

All the teams finished at the same time, discovering the spot where the treasure was hidden.

The blossom competition was the star event on the games schedule. Each team was given a flowering plant. Their challenge was to use their talents to make the plants blossom.

The teams rose to the challenge without further ado: Haunting melodies filled the air, with some of the fairies dancing around the plants and some gently caressing the leaves. Dandelions, anemones, bluebells, buttercups, primroses, and spectacular wild roses were lined up and bloomed in concert. The flowers radiated beauty and released their perfume into the air. The fairies – each in their teams – stood back and admired their handiwork, beaming with pleasure. Fired up by the shared experience, they exchanged tips and stories on how to get the best results, gorgeous blooms, luscious vegetables, flowers for the bees and so much more.

Their teachers looked on with pride and delight. They had been aiming for a valuable, shared experience for the teams for them to learn to like each other – but seeing the rapport between their students, how they engaged with each other and were learning from each other, was more than they had hoped for.

The fairies were too busy talking to notice their teachers' sudden disappearance...

Awards ceremony.

Dawn was breaking on the first day of May – "*Lá na Bealtaine*" – the day which marked the completion of the apprentice fairies' tasks.

They gathered in the grassy area bordered by trees and went to stand beside the Listening Tree. Their presence had been requested by their teachers, so there was some surprise when they discovered their teachers were absent. As on the day before, they were nowhere to be seen. Puzzled, the teams put their heads together to discuss their teachers' whereabouts.

In a moment, a sudden sharp gust of wind swished through the trees, whipping through the branches and sending the leaves all aquiver. One by one their teachers appeared in a soft halo of light that contrasted all the more with a blinding flash.

Whom did it reveal? You'll never guess so I will tell you: Conor, King of the fairies.

What was this all about, the fairies wondered. Nobody had mentioned that he was coming to the gala.

Síofra took to the air to find a height where everyone could see her. She began to speak: "My dear fairies, how wonderful that we can all be here together on this special day. This is your graduation ceremony when you transition from being apprentices to proper fairies. Allow me to congratulate you!"

A resounding cheer went up from the crowd of fairies. They were not alone, however. All the birds, foxes, squirrels, owls, and pigeons who had gathered to see this spectacle added their enthusiastic chirpings, hooting, and calls.

Síofra continued, "As you know, there can only ever be one winner. The accolade earned by the team of fairies who excelled. The prize goes to the team who showed the greatest kindness, included everyone and performed the best".

The fairies held their breath as she held up the trophy.

Naturally, each and every one of them wanted their team to win and had all done their utmost to be as good a team player as possible. But was it enough? They were well aware that some teams hadn't performed at their best on the obstacle course. But then they had evened that out by being really good at levitating.

Other teams had put in a superior performance at the treasure hunt but were unable to match the others in repairing the damaged tree. In heightened anticipation, they stood awaiting the verdict. Which team would win the treasured trophy?

Their attention was suddenly directed elsewhere: Conor, the King of the fairies described an elegant loop in the air and gracefully swooped down to join Síofra.

.

"My dear fairies", he addressed them from above in his velvety, booming voice

"This gala with its challenges presented you with the opportunity of proving your worth as good fairies and of showing what you have learned. What we saw here was how all of you – without exception – showed how keen you were to help each other.

Members of different teams stepped in to assist others whenever they could. Each and every one of you did a fine job in dealing with the challenges – and why? Because you all saw to it that no one was left behind or excluded no matter how different they looked, or how they spoke.

The differences between you ceased to matter and you essentially functioned as one team that worked beautifully together".

At his words, the teachers fluttered their wings in excitement and pride in their young fairies. Seeing this, Conor's face lit up and he smiled his magical smile. Síofra and the other teachers beamed back at him and then at their protégées.

What came next was totally unexpected: "I hereby announce", Connor declared, "that there can be no single winner!" With that, he waved his magic wand, and then, pointing it towards the earth, he conjured five identical trophies.

"Each team", he said, "will receive a trophy!"

The shouts of delight were so loud that they could be heard as far afield as Galway City, with all present participating in their own way.

The smaller birds broke into song, while the foxes and squirrels and other woodland animals danced in sheer joy, with the owls, pigeons, magpies, wrens and blackbirds flying in ever wider circles above the fairies who were celebrating enthusiastically with their teachers and their King.

Even the teachers gave each other hugs. It was a magical scene.

Finally

Merlin Woods was strangely quiet after the visiting teams had left. Naoise and Willow were sitting on a mossy rock reflecting on how it all went.

"That was an amazing gala, wasn't it?" said Willow.

"Oh yes, it was. Who would have thought it would turn out that way!" Naoise replied.

"It was so exciting that all our teams were each awarded a trophy – because we accepted each other, we included each other and embraced our differences.

I'd love to speak that mumbo-jumbo the Aranislians were taking. That way, if I ever get to visit their woods, I will be able to understand everything much better. They sure did look like they had lots of fun stories they could share with us!" Willow commented.

"Yeah! You know, I was quite stunned when I saw the different teams arriving. Their clothes were so different and they moved so peculiarly! The unfamiliar words they used and their strange skin colours! I found it all so confusing at first – took me right out of my comfort zone. But I am so very glad I stopped thinking like that.

Just imagine: if we had let our differences keep us apart, we would have lost the opportunity of achieving great things together, pooling our strengths paid off big time. Which team would have won? None of the teams were that great by themselves. Maybe no one would have the trophy let alone one for each of our teams!".

Willow laughed at that.

"You are so right. We felt free to join in because we accepted each other. I think no one should be judged by how they look or talk or act as long as they do no harm. Outward appearances really don't tell you how good or how kind they are inside".

The two fairies were quiet for a while just letting this sink in. Then Naoise said thoughtfully:

"Well, we have seen what's possible when we join together as one fairy family, all deserving of equal respect and treatment."

Naoise nodded wisely in agreement: "After all, if we were all the same, the world would be a very boring place!"

That made them laugh and, hugging each other happily, they both agreed this had been the best gala EVER!

The End

Discussion Points

What's a "normal" person? Is there such a thing?

What do you think about how the story unfolded?"

"How would you respond in the same situation?"

"Would this work in your school?"

If you were to see something that isn't fair, what would you do?

Did you know that everyone has a funny story to tell, has had something so exciting happen to them, has a favourite colour, and has a pet hate? Try asking! Try out new things ... like the fairies, go visit other woods.

Shouldn't we learn together about people from other places and cultures? What do you think? We can read books, watch movies, listen to music, and learn about celebrations that aren't part of our own traditions. We can attend cultural fairs and museums which highlight stories, art and the histories of people who are different from us. How enriching do you think that could be?

Fun Facts about Herbs

Learning about plants and herbs and what they can do for you can bring you on a magical journey.

Since the beginning of time, herbs are eaten or used to flavour foods. plants using their leaves, seeds or flowers. Some herbs can also be used as medicine.

In the past, people who helped cure others using herbs were considered to be witches with all their potions.

Let's look at some herbs that are how they can be used to help you.

Aloe The juice from the aloe plant soothes burns and sunburns. Some people drink aloe juice for a stomach ache.

Cinnamon kills viruses

Cloves helps get rid of a toothache

Garlic is good for the heart and helps fight infection, as it kills bacteria and gets rid of toxins in the body

Ginger eases stomach ache and nausea

Lavender can help you relax, as well as help you sleep

Oregano fights viruses and bacteria

Mint gets rid of gas and stomach aches. It also helps you to relax and rest

Arnica eases pain, prevents infection, is antibacterial and can heal wounds.

But the list is endless and every illness can be treated with different herbs or a combination of different herbs. There is an extensive amount that a person can do using herbs.

There are different ways you can use the herbs to help you. You can make teas, tinctures or pastes out of herbs. You can even take baths in herbal mixtures! You can make perfumes, soaps, hair rinses and lots more out of herbs. It all depends on what the problem is, that you are trying to solve.

Now here are a couple of old housewives' tricks:

The tops of parsley are eaten fresh to get rid of bad breath

A mixture of Oregano, Sage and Marjoram makes your Bolognese sauce really tasty.

Basil plants keep the flies away.

Cucumber can cool skin down.

Chopped onions on a plate by your bedside at night can help against chesty coughs.

Dock leaves can heal any stings especially nettle stings

Acknowledgements

I would like to express my heartfelt thanks to

Fionn and Kealan, my sons who have been my helpers throughout all my writing and musings.

Diana Polkinghorne, my dear friend, who bravely proofread and edited all these stories.

Terry O Flaherty, who has been a constant and tremendous support as well as a kind friend.

Emily Deavy, a kind friend and guiding light; a star.

Liam Begley, my big brother who has been such a great help throughout.

Therese Begley Luke, my sister, without whom none of these books would be possible.

Siobhan Conneely and Monique Moran, my Queenager buddies.

To my inspirational and endearing friend Susanna Lobina

And to my friends, Eliza, Karina, Susanna, Anca, Ljudmila, Gelika, Cemile, Mandy, and Brian Vibenholt.

About the Author

Martha Begley Schade is a writer and author of the highly acclaimed Galway Fairytales – Merlin Woods series.

 After years of working in business management, during which she had also written several books relative to her work, she has now put pen to paper to realize a lifelong dream of story-telling, a talent that was handed down through generations in her family.

With a B.Sc. in physics & maths, and an MBA, her new venture into children's storytelling comes from a lifelong passion of entertaining and educating children.

After 22 great years of living and working in Germany, she returned to Galway in 2008 with her two sons. The only place she ever wanted to live, she finds the Tribes people are the kindest and most caring she has ever met.

With the sea air, the seagulls flying overhead, the buzz of the city, the glistening beaches and beautiful hills of Connemara, all combine to only cement her love for her adopted home.

Merlin Fairy Series

Liam & Carmie. Apologies Matter!

Síofra & Her Apprentices. Developing A Social Conscience.

The Fairy Gala. Community Includes Everyone.

Dubheasa & Fiadh. Breaking Up is Hard To Do.

Mary & Macriona. Coping With Anxiety.

Irish stories about fairies from Merlin Woods who learn from their mistakes or through their life experiences. From the fox Liam who steals the fairy Carmie's food and has to learn how to apologise, to the teacher Síofra who has difficulties teaching responsibility to her apprentices, to the fairies learning to appreciate the differences in others. Then there are the fairies whose family home breaks up and the fairy Macriona who suffers from anxiety. All stories are educational and culminate with positive endings.

The Merlin Fairy Compilation book has all five books of the series.

Order Your Books Here:

©www.galwayfairytales.com

Merlin Woods Series

Flappy. The Pigeon Who Overcame Bullying

Billa & Buster. The Circle Of Kindness

Golden Key of Wisdom. A journey into Teamwork

The Listening Tree. Befriending Nature

Emily & Tristan. How Friends Can Make A difference

Charming and educational stories about animal characters living in Merlin Woods in Galway, who find their way through difficult topics that children have to face nowadays.

Crafted stories about a pigeon who is bullied, seven squirrels who overcome obstacles to become a great team, the cat who changes the life of her friend the depressed owl, a girl's lifelong friendship with a tree and an abandoned puppy who finds the value of kindness through friendship with a badger.

The Merlin Woods Compilation book has all five books of the series.

Order Your Books Here:

©www.galwayfairytales.com